NEW BELIEVER'S GUIDE TO
Prayer

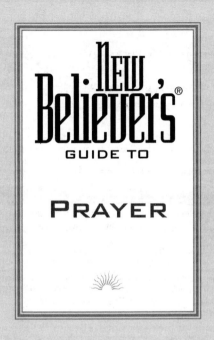

New Believer's® GUIDE TO

PRAYER

GREG LAURIE

TYNDALE HOUSE PUBLISHERS, INC.
WHEATON, ILLINOIS

Visit Tyndale's exciting Web site at www.tyndale.com

New Believer's Guide to Prayer

Copyright © 2003 by Greg Laurie. All rights reserved.

Designed by Kelly Bennema

Edited by L. B. Norton

Library of Congress Cataloging-in-Publication Data

Laurie, Greg.
  New believer's guide to prayer / Greg Laurie with Linda
Taylor.
     p. cm.
ISBN 0-8423-5572-3
1. Prayer—Christianity. I. Taylor, Linda Chaffee, date. II. Title.
BV210.3 .L38 2003
248.3′2—dc21   2002014262

Printed in the United States of America

08   07   06   05   04   03
8   7   6   5   4   3   2

Contents

1

THE POWER OF PRAYER

Have you ever been in an impossible situation, with no way out? Have you ever desperately wanted something but knew there was no way you could ever have it? Have you ever thought there's no future for you—that you're hopeless and it's too late to change?

If you've had such thoughts and feelings, you're not alone. Many people feel trapped by life's circumstances, unable to cope, thinking they can't go on. They need someone they can talk to, someone they can count on, someone to give them hope.

As a new believer in Jesus Christ, you've found the One who can give you that hope. You are in the process of learning that

- nothing is impossible with God;
- God can fulfill your needs (and sometimes even your dreams);
- you do have a future and a hope—it's never too late.

You are also learning that you can call on the Lord 24/7—which is to say, all day every day, from any place, for any reason. The way you do that is through prayer.

By prayer we come into God's presence. By prayer we talk to Him—about anything and everything. Just as you can talk over anything with a good friend, so you can call on God under any circumstances, for any reason.

Let's look at some examples from the Bible of people who knew when to pray. Each of them experienced the power of prayer firsthand. From their stories you will observe that prayer can dramatically change situations, people, and sometimes even the course of nature.

When Things Look Impossible

Did you ever face something that felt just too big to handle? Did it seem like the odds were stacked against you and there was no way out? Take a chapter from the life of Old Testament king Jehoshaphat, who was doing the best he could when, without warning, the bottom dropped out of his life (see 2 Chronicles 19–20).

Jehoshaphat was one of the few good kings to reign over the southern kingdom of Judah. Despite a few slipups, he tried to follow the Lord and bring his nation back to the worship of God by destroying the idols that had been built in his land.

Then one day he received word that a "vast army" of Moabites, Ammonites, and Meunites—much larger than the army he commanded—was marching against Judah. The odds were definitely against him.

The Bible tells us that Jehoshaphat was "alarmed." I should think so. But the first thing he did was turn to the Lord for guidance. Instead of worrying, he did just as the apostle Paul, centuries later, would instruct the church at Philippi: "Don't worry about anything; instead, pray about everything. Tell God what you need, and thank him for all he has done" (Philippians 4:6). Jehoshaphat took his "alarm" to God and sought His guidance.

Read the king's prayer in 2 Chronicles 20:5-12. In so many words he said, "Okay, God, You gave this land to us as a promise to Abraham. Then when our ancestors came here, You told us not to destroy the Moabites and Ammonites and the people of Mount Seir. In fact, if You remember, You told us not to even travel through their lands but to go the long way around! So we did as You said and left those people alone, and *now they are the ones coming to attack us!*"

Of course, God already knew all this, but Jehoshaphat laid out the situation before Him. Listen to Jehoshaphat's request: "O our God, won't you stop them? We are powerless against this mighty army that is about to attack us. We do not know what to do, but we are looking to you for help" (v. 12).

And God did indeed help. God responded power-fully, answering the prayer of the king and his people. Just read what happened in verses 13-30.

When you have an "impossible" need, remember that "nothing is impossible with God" (Luke 1:37). Talk to Him about it. He may not answer all your questions. He may not answer as quickly as he answered Jehoshaphat. Then again, He might! But you will have taken your need to the only One who can truly help, the almighty Creator of the universe. What more could you need?

When You Have a Desire

Did you ever desire something very much? Sometimes the things we desire are not good for us, and God knows it, so He says no to a request. Sometimes the things we desire are good but not good at that particular time, so He tells us to wait. At other times He sees our pure hearts and motivations and answers with a resounding "yes," as He did with Hannah (see 1 Samuel 1).

Hannah was an Israelite who was unable to have children. Infertility is difficult and painful enough for women today, but in Hannah's day, it was considered a curse. To make matters worse, Hannah's husband had another wife who *was* able to have children, and she made fun of Hannah's infertility. Hannah's husband loved her very much, but she still wanted to have a child.

Hannah took her request to God. You can read her prayer in 1 Samuel 1:11: "O Lord Almighty, if you will look down upon my sorrow and answer my prayer and give me a son, then I will give him back to you. He will be yours for his entire lifetime, and as a sign that he has been dedicated to the Lord, his hair will never be cut."

God answered Hannah's prayer, and her child, Samuel, grew up to be a prophet who helped to heal the nation of Israel after the chaotic years under the judges.

Jesus promises that when our requests are in line with God's will, He will hear and answer. "You can ask for anything in my name, and I will do it, because the work of the Son brings glory to the Father. Yes, ask anything in my name, and I will do it!" (John 14:13-14).

Now this does not necessarily mean you can ask for whatever you want and God will give it to you. The key is to discover the will of God and pray accordingly. Your requests will more likely be in line with His will when you are in tune with Him—learning about Him and what He wants you to do, obeying Him, and following Him. Then you can bring any and every request to God, trusting Him to do His will.

When It Seems Too Late

Can you pray even after you've messed things up? Of course—otherwise God couldn't have listened to that first prayer you prayed in order to be saved. Sometimes we fail, but God is always ready to hear, forgive, and set us back on the right path to serve Him. If you find that hard to believe, take a look at the story of Samson (see Judges 13–16).

Samson had great potential. Like Hannah, Samson's mother had been unable to have children, but then an angel promised her a son (Judges 13:5). Her child would be very great and would "rescue Israel from the Philistines." Samson would be set aside for this special task and be a Nazirite—meaning he would have to keep certain vows during his lifetime, including never cutting his hair.

God did indeed use Samson's mighty strength to harass the Philistines, but unfortunately, Samson did not stay close to the Lord. He got involved with a Philistine woman named Delilah and told her the secret of his great strength: "'My hair has never been cut,' he confessed, 'for I was dedicated to God as a Nazirite from birth. If my head were shaved, my strength would leave me, and I would become as weak as anyone else'" (Judges 16:17).

Delilah told Samson's secret to the Philistine leaders who had been desperately trying to find a way to stop his constant harassment. Delilah lulled Samson to sleep, cut his hair, and called in his enemies, who put him in chains, blinded him, and put him in prison.

But even after Samson's failure, God gave him another chance. The Philistines held a great celebration to thank their god for delivering Samson to them. They brought him out for entertainment, chaining him between two big pillars in their temple. Samson prayed, "Sovereign Lord, remember me again. O God, please strengthen me one more time so that I may pay back the Philistines for the loss of my eyes" (Judges 16:28).

And God answered his prayer. He gave Samson the strength to push over the pillars he was chained to and literally bring down the house! In the end, Samson played a part in God's plan to deliver his nation from the Philistines.

Satan knows that prayer is your lifeline to God. When you have sinned, Satan whispers in your ear, "Do you think God hears the prayers of someone like you? You are such a failure and hypocrite. Don't even think about praying!"

It is easy to fall for a ploy like that. But the truth is that when you have sinned, *that* is the time to pray! Your first prayer should be one of repentance, in which you acknowledge your wrongdoing and turn from it. Then, like Samson, you should ask God for another chance. He will graciously give it to you.

When You Don't Understand

We don't understand all that happens in our lives. We don't see the "big picture" that God sees, so there are plenty of things we wonder about. But take your questions to God and place them in His capable hands. He wants you to trust Him even when you don't understand.

Paul and Silas were taking the gospel message to people who had never heard it. God had sent them a vision to go into an area called Macedonia. The first place they visited was the city of Philippi. And what happened? They ended up stripped, beaten, flogged, and thrown into prison. They were put into the inner dungeon with their feet in stocks.

Now wait a minute! Weren't they doing just what God had called them to do? Yes, they were. And they were right where God wanted them at the moment. Content in that knowledge, what were Paul and Silas doing in that dark prison cell? Praying and singing hymns to God! (See Acts 16:25.)

The Bible doesn't tell us the words of their prayers, but we can guess that they weren't despairing cries of fear—not when they were also singing! Paul and Silas trusted God to do what He desired with them, for they were in His hands. They didn't understand, but they prayed.

A similar situation had occurred with the apostle Peter a few years earlier. He too had been imprisoned for teaching the gospel—doing just what God had called him to do. His fellow apostle James had just been killed by Herod for the same reason, and now Peter was on death row. And do you know what he was doing in prison? The Bible tells us he was sleeping! Not sitting awake wringing his hands, worried, scared—he was sleeping.

But I imagine that he had done plenty of praying

first, and the Bible tells us that other people were praying "very earnestly" for him as well. The church didn't understand God's ways; in fact, they may have questioned them. But they didn't stop praying. And Peter was miraculously set free! (Read his story in Acts 12:1-17.)

When You Feel Alone

You may never be imprisoned for your faith, but that doesn't mean you don't have problems. Do you ever feel all alone—just you against the world? No one to turn to? No one who understands? Do you ever feel a sort of darkness overwhelm you with fear and depression?

Elijah is a Bible hero who understands those feelings. A powerful prophet of God, Elijah was used in mighty ways to speak God's words to the string of evil kings that ruled the northern kingdom of Israel. He made himself plenty of enemies along the way, because he always brought bad news. (That's because the people were sinning against God—but they never made the connection!)

Perhaps Elijah is most famous for his contest with the prophets of the false god Baal on Mount Carmel. Jezebel, the queen of Israel, employed hundreds of false prophets, and Elijah invited them to a contest: "Now bring all the people of Israel to Mount Carmel, with all 450 prophets of Baal and the 400 prophets of

Asherah, who are supported by Jezebel" (1 Kings 18:19).

Imagine that! Setting up a contest where the odds are 850 to 1 against you! But Elijah knew that the contest was not really between him and those prophets but between God and a powerless idol. Obviously, this was no contest at all. Elijah prayed to God to send down fire from heaven to show the people of Israel who was really God—and God answered. Then Elijah prayed that God would end a seven-year drought by bringing rain—and God answered.

But then Queen Jezebel put a price on Elijah's head, and he ran for his life. "He went on alone into the desert, traveling all day. He sat down under a solitary broom tree and prayed that he might die. 'I have had enough, Lord,' he said. 'Take my life, for I am no better than my ancestors'" (1 Kings 19:4). His biggest complaint was that he thought he was the only worshiper of God in the entire kingdom. Elijah told God his true feelings. God listened, let Elijah rest a bit, fed him, told him the truth, and then sent him back to work.

We can pray to God even when we feel the worst. In fact, He is the best One for us to go to. He understands, He answers, and He gets us going again.

Great Power, Wonderful Results

Some people ask, "Do I have to pray in a certain position to know I'll be answered?" Three ministers were debating this question. One minister shared that he felt the key was in the hands. He always held his hands together and pointed them upward as a symbolic form of worship.

Another minister suggested that real prayer was conducted on your knees. That was the only way to really pray.

The third said that they were both wrong. The only position in which to pray was to lie on the floor flat on your face.

As they were talking, a telephone repairman had been working in the background, overhearing their conversation. Finally, he could take it no longer. He blurted, "I found that the most powerful prayer I ever prayed was while I was dangling upside down by my heels from a power pole suspended forty feet above the ground!"

As we saw from the biblical examples in this chapter, we can pray in any position, anytime, anywhere. And remember Jonah, who prayed from the belly of a fish (see Jonah 2:1). God will hear your prayer wherever you are.

Without any mention of when, where, or how, the apostle James says to his readers, "The earnest prayer of a righteous person has great power and wonderful results" (James 5:16). As believers we are considered "righteous persons" even though we know we're not perfect yet. God sees us as "righteous" because He has forgiven us. So our prayers have great power and wonderful results.

We can communicate with God about any situation, at any time, in any way. He promises to hear and answer. He's just waiting to hear from you.

Do you have anything you need to pray about right now? A problem at work or school or with family or friends? Perhaps you need a healing touch from God. Maybe you need His wisdom for a certain situation. Talk to your loving heavenly Father about it. He's only a prayer away!

2

LORD, TEACH ME TO PRAY

The disciples observed Jesus' habit of going away to pray (sometimes all night). At one point, when He returned to them, they made this request of Him: "Lord, teach us to pray" (Luke 11:1).

Perhaps that is your request today. "Lord, teach me to pray." In the previous chapter we looked at people in the Bible who prayed for a variety of reasons. Because prayer is simply communication with our Friend, our Father, our King, we can talk to Him about anything. That's what Jesus did—and He is our ultimate example.

While Jesus was on earth, He talked to His Father through prayer. They were in constant communication. Look at what the following verses tell us about Jesus' habit of prayer:

The next morning Jesus awoke long before daybreak and went out alone into the wilderness to pray. (Mark 1:35)

Afterward he went up into the hills by himself to pray. (Mark 6:46)

One day soon afterward Jesus went to a moun-
tain to pray, and he prayed to God all night.
(Luke 6:12)

Jesus took time to talk to His Father. He often went off alone, where He would not be distracted or interrupted. Prayer was a vital part of His time on this earth. If Jesus took the time to talk with His Father, how much more should we!

The Prayer Jesus Taught His Disciples

The prayer Jesus taught His disciples was not necessarily meant to be prayed verbatim, although there is nothing wrong with doing that. But just before He gave them this prayer He told them: "When you pray, do not use vain repetitions as the heathen do. For they think that they will be heard for their many words" (Matthew 6:7, NKJV). In other words, this prayer wasn't meant to be the *only* prayer they could ever pray—otherwise it would have become no more than vain repetition. Instead, it is a pattern for the way Jesus' followers can approach their heavenly Father in prayer. It is not *what* we have to pray but a template that shows *how* we should pray.

Listen to what Jesus said:

This, then, is how you should pray:
"Our Father in heaven,
hallowed be your name,

> *your kingdom come,*
> *your will be done*
> *on earth as it is in heaven.*
> *Give us today our daily bread.*
> *Forgive us our debts,*
> *as we also have forgiven our debtors.*
> *And lead us not into temptation,*
> *but deliver us from the evil one."*

Matthew 6:9-13, NIV

This prayer can be divided into two parts. The first deals with God's glory, the second with our needs. We will look at each phrase separately and discuss what it means regarding our own prayers.

"Our Father in heaven, hallowed be your name"

The beginning of this prayer is noteworthy. To call God "our Father" was a revolutionary thought to the disciples. As Jews, they feared God and attached such sacredness to His name that they wouldn't even utter it! But when Jesus went to the cross to die for our sins, He brought us back into a relationship with God. As He said to Mary Magdalene after His resurrection, "I am ascending to my Father and your Father, my God and your God" (John 20:17).

God is not some distant, unapproachable being. He wants to draw close to us, and He wants us to draw close to Him. The Bible tells us, "You should not be like cowering, fearful slaves. You should behave instead like God's very own children, adopted into his family—calling him 'Father, dear Father' " (Romans 8:15).

The word *hallowed* could also be translated *holy*. God is holy, meaning He is totally and completely perfect, separate from all that is sinful. Because we are sinful beings, there was no way for us to ever have a relationship with Him. That's why Jesus had to come—as a human, but without sin—in order to bridge the gap between us and God. It is vital that we remember this awesome and holy God is also our loving Father. He can be both because of what Jesus did in taking our place on the cross and paying for our sins. On the cross, God treated Jesus as if He had personally committed every sin ever committed by every person who would ever live—even though He had committed none of them. Because of this, His righteousness has been placed into our spiritual bank account.

As our loving heavenly Father, God has our best interests at heart. God is all-powerful, all-knowing, and present everywhere. That means He is unlimited in power, ignorant of nothing, and not bound by time or space. He is just, good, righteous, and loving. His decisions and purposes are always right and proper, always motivated by a pure goodness and a deep and abiding love for us.

The fact that you and I could even have the privilege of approaching a God like this is staggering. Yet when Jesus instructed His disciples to pray, He didn't say, "Our God in heaven," but "Our *Father* in heaven." The all-powerful, all-knowing, present-everywhere, holy, righteous, good, and loving Creator of the entire universe is "our Father in heaven"!

Through the structure of this prayer, Jesus is showing us that when we pray, we should not immediately come to God with our wants or even our needs. Instead, we should first contemplate the greatness and glory of our Father.

"Your kingdom come"

Contained in these words is a multilevel request with different shades of meaning. First of all, this is a request for Jesus' return to earth. The word that Jesus uses here for *kingdom* does not refer primarily to a geographical territory but to sovereignty and dominion. Therefore, when we pray "your kingdom come," we are praying for God's rule on earth, which essentially begins when Jesus returns to rule and reign.

The word *come* indicates a sudden, instantaneous coming. In essence, we're saying, "Lord, please come back . . . and do it soon!"

Is your spiritual life in such a place right now where you can pray this? The ability to truly say that you want Jesus to return is an indicator of where you are with God. The person who is walking with God daily will also be longing for His return.

A second aspect of this request is personal. When we say, "your kingdom come," we are asking for the kingdom of God to come in our own lives. When Jesus walked the earth, He said, "The Kingdom of God has arrived among you" (Matthew 12:28). He was referring to His presence.

As a new believer, you know that Jesus Himself has taken up residence in your life. When you pray this prayer, you're saying that you want Jesus to rule and reign in your life and that you want to live by the principles found in His Word. You want Him to be in charge; you're giving Him the master key to every room in your life.

When you pray "your kingdom come," you're also praying "my kingdom go," for there cannot be two kingdoms ruling in your life. Praying "your kingdom come" is saying, "Lord, if what I am about to pray for is in any way outside of your will, then overrule it."

Another facet of this phrase encompasses a request for the salvation of those who don't know the Lord. As His kingdom is ruling and reigning in our own lives, we can play a part in bringing it to others as well. God's kingdom is brought to this earth each time a new soul is brought to Jesus. Thus, "your kingdom come" is also an evangelistic prayer. We are praying for the rule and reign of Jesus in the lives of many others. This is a reminder that we should be praying for the salvation of those who do not yet know the Lord.

"Your will be done on earth as it is in heaven"
To want God's will to be done means that we need to seek to align our will with His. Then we will see our prayers answered in the affirmative.

There is no doubt that it is the will of God that people come to believe in Jesus Christ. The Bible tells us, "[The Lord] does not want anyone to perish" (2 Peter 3:9). God's desire is to save people. Isaiah 53:12 prophesies about Jesus that He "interceded for sinners." On the cross He prayed for His murderers, "Father, forgive these people, because they don't know what they are doing" (Luke 23:34).

A striking illustration of prayer for nonbelievers is shown in the story of Stephen, the first Christian martyr. The Jewish leaders stoned him to death because of his uncompromising stand for Jesus. Yet even as he was dying, he said, "Lord, do not hold this sin against them" (Acts 7:60, NIV). The next chapter in Acts tells us that a young man was watching the execution that day—even holding the coats of those who were throwing the stones. His name was Saul (or, in Greek, Paul). He would soon become a Christian himself and would change the world for Christ. That makes me wonder: Could Stephen, inspired by the Holy Spirit, have been praying specifically for Saul? When Saul became a Christian, it was such an astounding surprise that most people did not believe it. Some even thought he was pretending to be converted in order to find even more Christians and turn them over to the Jewish leaders.

Clearly, God loves to save people—and He sometimes does it in the most amazing ways to the most surprising people. Do you know someone right now whom you cannot even imagine being a Christian? Start praying for that person! Pray for God's will to be done, on earth as it is in heaven. Pray that God's will—that all would be saved—will be made a reality in the life of this person. Of course, the final outcome will lie with God, but it is certainly God's will that we pray this way.

"Give us today our daily bread"

It is really amazing to consider that the all-knowing, all-powerful, present-everywhere God who created the entire universe could have any personal interest in us. Job wondered the same thing when he said, "What is man that you make so much of him, that you give him so much attention?" (Job 7:17, NIV). Why would God be concerned about what concerns us? Why would He care about our needs—and even our wants? Why would He commit Himself personally to providing our "daily bread"?

Many reasons could be cited, but the most notable is simply that He loves us! Jesus told His followers, "Don't be afraid, little flock. For it gives your Father great happiness to give you the Kingdom" (Luke 12:32).

"Give us today our daily bread" is not only a request; it is also an affirmation that everything we have ultimately comes from God. James wrote, "Every good gift and every perfect gift is from above, and comes down from the Father of lights, with whom there is no variation or shadow of turning" (James 1:17, NKJV). Every good gift is from Him!

Yes, we can work hard, save, and wisely invest our money, but the very ability to do this comes from God. "It is He who gives you power to get wealth" (Deuteronomy 8:18, NKJV). In this prayer, Jesus gives us permission to ask God to provide for us—because everything we already have came from Him. God Almighty has committed Himself to personally meeting the needs of His children. The Bible assures us, "Since God did not spare even his own Son but gave him up for us all, won't God, who gave us Christ, also give us everything else?" (Romans 8:32).

Of course, this doesn't mean that we can sit around like lazy bums and say, "Give me my daily bread, Lord!" The Bible also says that those who don't work shouldn't eat (see 2 Thessalonians 3:10). We must be diligent to do our part, working hard, putting in an honest day's work. To pray for God's provision of our daily bread is to recognize God as the Provider, even as we work for our bread. We do our part, and God promises to do His.

"Forgive us our debts, as we also have forgiven our debtors"

I once heard of a minister who, short of time and unable to find a parking space, left his car in a No Parking zone. He put a note under the windshield wiper that read, "I have circled the block ten times. I have an appointment to keep. 'Forgive us our debts.'" When he returned, he found a citation from a police officer along with this note: "I've circled this block for ten years. If I don't give you a ticket, I could lose my job. 'Lead us not into temptation.'"

What are our "debts"? The word translated *debts* could also be translated as sins, trespasses, shortcomings, resentments, what we owe to someone, or a wrong we've done.

Some people think they don't need forgiveness. But according to this model prayer, forgiveness is something we should request on a regular basis. "If we say we have no sin, we are only fooling ourselves and refusing to accept the truth" (1 John 1:8). People who do not see a constant need for regular cleansing from sin are not spending much time in God's presence.

Of course, when you accepted Jesus as your Savior, He washed away all your sin and freed you from its stranglehold. However, while you are still in this life, you will battle with your sin nature. The greater the saint, the greater is the sense of sin and the awareness of sin within. The great apostle Paul described the battle:

> *I don't understand myself at all, for I really want to do what is right, but I don't do it. Instead, I do the very thing I hate. I know perfectly well that what I am doing is wrong, and my bad conscience shows that I agree that the law is good. But I can't help myself, because it is sin inside me that makes me do these evil things. I know I am rotten through and through so far as my old sinful nature is concerned. No matter which way I turn, I can't make myself do right. I want to, but I can't. When I want to do good, I don't. And when I try not to do wrong, I do it anyway. But if I am doing what I don't want to do, I am not really the one doing it; the sin within me is doing it. It seems to be a fact of life that when I want to do what is right, I inevitably do what is wrong. (Romans 7:15-21)*

Is that how you feel sometimes? That's because your sin nature is still very much a part of you. You will continue to sin, but you can always come to God for forgiveness and cleansing.

Because we have been forgiven, we should willingly extend forgiveness to others. Think about how many movies and TV programs you have seen where the basic premise is this: the good guy gets hurt, the good guy regroups, the good guy pulverizes the bad guy. When is the last time you saw a program where the good guy gets hurt and then *forgives* the bad guy? Are you kidding? It doesn't happen!

Society doesn't seem to take kindly to forgiveness. It values vengeance instead. In our culture we firmly believe the adage, "Don't get mad, get even!"

As fatally flawed people, we are going to sin. We are going to hurt one another, whether intentionally or unintentionally. But according to Jesus, *forgiven* people should be *forgiving* people. In many ways, forgiveness is the key to all relationships that are healthy, strong, and lasting.

Jesus was speaking on the topic of forgiveness when Peter asked, "'Lord, how often should I forgive someone who sins against me? Seven times?' 'No!' Jesus replied, 'seventy times seven!'" (Matthew 18:21-22). Peter really thought he was being generous to offer to forgive someone seven times. But Jesus said that we should be willing to forgive 490 times! In other words, don't even keep count. Just keep on forgiving. The number of times the other person sins is the number of times you should forgive.

"But," you may protest, "the person doesn't deserve forgiveness!" Did *you* deserve to be forgiven by God?

That's right. You don't deserve forgiveness either. But God forgave you anyway. That's the kind of forgiveness Jesus expects us to extend to others. Paul put it this way: "Be kind to each other, tenderhearted, forgiving one another, just as God through Christ has forgiven you" (Ephesians 4:32).

"Lead us not into temptation, but deliver us from the evil one"

This phrase does not mean that God would lead us into temptation. In fact, the Bible also says, "Remember, no one who wants to do wrong should ever say, 'God is tempting me.' God is never tempted to do wrong, and he never tempts anyone else either. Temptation comes from the lure of our own evil desires. These evil desires lead to evil actions, and evil actions lead to death" (James 1:13-15).

When we pray for God not to lead us into temptation, we are asking God to guide us so that we will not get out of His will and place ourselves in the way of temptation. We're saying, "Lord, don't let me be tempted above my capacity to resist."

Temptation itself is not a sin. Jesus Himself was tempted, and Jesus never sinned. Our problem with temptation, of course, is that we can rationalize giving in to it. Sometimes we don't see temptation for what it is until it's too late. That's where we need God's help—and that's why we need to pray these words. If we could see our own temptations as clearly as we see other people's, they wouldn't be that hard to identify. Other people's temptations look so ugly and foolish that we say, "How could they do that?" Yet somehow ours seem different, acceptable, justifiable. We think, "My case is different." Then one day our house of cards collapses, and we see our sin for what it really is.

Here's a litmus test to apply when you are not sure if something is a temptation (an enticement to evil). First, pray about it and bring it into the clear light of God's presence. When you're not sure, ask, "Should I allow myself to be in this potentially vulnerable situation? Lord, if this is not pleasing to you, let me know, and I'll get out of here!" If you don't *want* to pray about something, chances are you already know the answer. When you are following your Father in heaven, who is holy (as acknowledged at the beginning of this prayer), then you will begin to see things as they really are.

A second thing you should do is ask yourself, "How would this look if some other Christian gave in to it?" If you saw another Christian doing what you are thinking of doing, how would you react?

You see, God knows how dangerous temptation is. It is so—well—tempting! Satan knows that if he can just give us a *taste*, he can get us hooked. It's like trying to eat just one potato chip or one freshly baked cookie. So we need God to help us steer clear of temptation.

What makes resisting temptation difficult for many people is that they don't try to avoid it completely. They want to be delivered from temptation without giving up the very things that put them in the path of temptation. To pray for protection against temptation and then rush into places of vulnerability is to thrust your fingers into the fire and hope they don't get burnt.

When Jesus told us to pray this way, He wanted us to always have before us our vulnerability to temptation and our need for vigilance. When we pray "lead us not into temptation," we are saying, "Lord, I know my own sinful vulnerabilities, and I ask you to keep me from the power of sin. Help me to make the right choices and avoid anything that would pull me away from you." This is an appeal to God to watch over our eyes, our ears, our mouth, our feet, our hands. We are asking that in whatever we see, hear, or say, in any place we go, and in anything we do, He will protect us from sin. We are laying claim to the promise recorded in 1 Corinthians 10:13:

> *Remember that the temptations that come into your life are no different from what others experience. And God is faithful. He will keep the temptation from becoming so strong that you can't stand up against it. When you are tempted, he will show you a way out so that you will not give in to it.*

This part of the Lord's Prayer is asking God to show us that "way out."

Jesus taught that we should always approach God

recognizing His awesome greatness. We should worship and adore Him. We should pray for His perfect will and the rule of His kingdom in our lives and in the lives of others. Then, after getting things into the proper perspective, we should bring our personal needs before Him.

In the next chapter we'll consider how to use this pattern in our personal prayers.

3

CONVERSING WITH GOD

I heard a story of a woman in Florida who fended off a would-be rapist with the Lord's Prayer. When she was attacked, she began to recite the words of that prayer in rapid-fire fashion. Her attacker covered his face with his hands and started shaking. As she repeated the prayer, he let her go and fled. Later the woman said that a peace came over her as she started praying the Lord's Prayer. She prayed to be delivered from evil, and she was!

How to Pray

The Lord's Prayer is a powerful prayer. You should seek to memorize and use it, but remember that it shouldn't be the only prayer you ever pray.

In chapter 2 we examined the meaning of each phrase. But how do you use this prayer as a pattern for your private time with the Lord?

I once learned a helpful acronym that can remind us how to pray. (Of course, God listens to all of our prayers—even the ones that don't follow this pattern!) The word is ACTS, and the letters stand for

Adoration

Confession

Thanksgiving

Supplication

Adoration

As in the Lord's Prayer, you can begin your prayer time by "adoring" God. This helps you remember that God is not a cosmic vending machine but deserves to be approached with reverence and awe. Maybe you think you don't have a whole lot to say, but start by acknowledging His greatness, power, and majesty. As the psalmist said, "Oh, magnify the Lord with me, and let us exalt His name together" (Psalm 34:3, NKJV). When we see God for who He is, we begin to see our problems for what they are.

In the book of Acts, the believers were told they could no longer preach the gospel. Instead of cowering in fear, they prayed. And they began their prayer by worshiping God and reflecting on His Word, thereby putting their considerable problems into the proper perspective:

> Then all the believers were united as they lifted their voices in prayer: "O Sovereign Lord, Creator of heaven and earth, the sea, and everything in them—you spoke long ago by the Holy Spirit through our ancestor King David, your servant,

saying, 'Why did the nations rage? Why did the people waste their time with futile plans? The kings of the earth prepared for battle; the rulers gathered together against the Lord and against his Messiah.' That is what has happened here in this city! For Herod Antipas, Pontius Pilate the governor, the Gentiles, and the people of Israel were all united against Jesus, your holy servant, whom you anointed. In fact, everything they did occurred according to your eternal will and plan." (Acts 4:24-28)

Having considered all that God had done in the past, they came to the problem at hand.

And now, O Lord, hear their threats, and give your servants great boldness in their preaching. Send your healing power; may miraculous signs and wonders be done through the name of your holy servant Jesus. After this prayer, the building where they were meeting shook, and they were all filled with the Holy Spirit. And they preached God's message with boldness. (Acts 4:29-31)

They began their prayer with adoration, got their problem into perspective, then made their request with boldness. And God answered!

Confession

When you became a Christian, Jesus washed away all

your sin. But you will soon discover (if you haven't already) that you still commit sin. The difference now is that you have an avenue for forgiveness in your relationship with God. When you come to Him in prayer, truly acknowledging and adoring Him, you will become painfully aware of your own weakness and vulnerability.

You need to take your sins to God and let Him forgive them. You see, if your relationship with God is like a fine piece of machinery, then sin is like a grain of sand that gets in and mucks up the gears. To pray for God's will to be done and to be in tune with what He wants, you need to deal with sin on a daily basis. The great thing is this: God promises that when we confess, He forgives—always:

> *If we confess our sins, he is faithful and just and will forgive us our sins and purify us from all unrighteousness. (1 John 1:9, NIV)*

Besides, confession is good for us:

> *Finally, I confessed all my sins to you and stopped trying to hide them. I said to myself, "I will confess my rebellion to the Lord." And you forgave me! All my guilt is gone. (Psalm 32:5)*

That's why confession is so vital in your relationship with God. Ask God to show you any wrongs that need to be cleansed. Maybe you already know them—

tell God. He already knows anyway, and He promises to forgive.

Thanksgiving

This is just what it sounds like. So often when we pray, we have a list of things we want God to do. However, if we follow the ACTS pattern, we first think about everything God has already done. Before you present your requests, what can you thank God for?

Look again at Paul and Silas, praising God before God's deliverance came:

> *They were severely beaten, and then they were thrown into prison. The jailer was ordered to make sure they didn't escape. So he took no chances but put them into the inner dungeon and clamped their feet in the stocks. Around mid-night, Paul and Silas were praying and singing hymns to God, and the other prisoners were listening.* (Acts 16:23-25)

How could they do such a thing under such difficult circumstances? They weren't necessarily in a position where one might think about being thankful, but they did it anyway. They knew that even in that awful dungeon they were right in the center of God's will. So they thanked Him for being with them.

Prayers of thanks were a part of Old Testament leader Nehemiah's lifestyle too. (You'll learn more about him later in this chapter.) When the people were rebuilding the walls of Jerusalem, he led them in prayers and songs of thankfulness to God:

> *I led the leaders of Judah to the top of the wall and organized two large choirs to give thanks. . . . The two choirs that were giving thanks then proceeded to the Temple of God, where they took their places. So did I, together with the group of leaders who were with me. (Nehemiah 12:31, 40)*

So after you've adored God and confessed your sin, take a few minutes for "T"—Thanksgiving. You'll discover so many things to be thankful for, and you'll be humbled to realize all that God has done and is doing for you every day.

Supplication

This is really just a fancy word for *asking*, but it also includes the elements of humility and honesty. And once you've adored God, confessed your sin, and thanked Him for all He has done for you, how could you be anything other than humble and honest? Your requests will naturally come from a humble heart.

It may help you to keep a list of ongoing prayer requests—things you want to pray about. Some people have prayer notebooks divided into the days of the week. They spread their regular requests (such as prayers for family and friends) across those days so each request gets made once a week.

It is also helpful to keep a written list of special prayer requests. In one column write the date you start praying for a specific request, and in another column write the date of God's answer. It may seem strange now, but over time you'll begin to see a whole column of requests and a whole column of answers. This becomes a strong encouragement to continue to pray for your own needs and the needs of others.

These verses from the Psalms may also encourage you:

> *The Lord has heard my supplication, the Lord receives my prayer. (Psalm 6:9, NASB)*

> *I love the Lord, because He hears my voice and my supplications. (Psalm 116:1, NASB)*

> *Let my supplication come before Thee; deliver me according to Thy word. (Psalm 119:170, NASB)*

Wind up your prayer with supplication, presenting your requests to God. He will receive your prayer, hear your voice, and deliver you, just as His Word promises.

Attitudes for Prayer

The communication you have with God should be like the communication you have with a friend—direct, honest, frequent. Yet unlike a friend, God is never too sensitive for our questions or too busy to talk to us or too sentimental to tell us what we may need to hear. We can pray about anything, anytime, with confidence and boldness, knowing that God will answer.

Be Honest

If you ever think you can hide something from God, you're in for a big surprise. He knows you completely. He knows your fears, your weaknesses, your strengths, your worries. No matter how you appear to others on the outside, God knows your motives.

When Jesus was in the garden of Gethsemane facing the most difficult hours of His earthly life, He asked His disciples to pray. He knew that He needed strength for the coming hours, but He knew they needed it too. And it was strength that could not possibly come from within themselves but would have to come from God. So He said to them, "Pray that you will not be overcome by temptation" (Luke 22:40).

For the disciples, the temptation would be to run away, to deny ever knowing anything about Jesus— temptation they pretty much all gave in to one way or another.

But Jesus' advice is helpful for all of us on a daily basis. You will face temptation—being a believer doesn't make it any less tempting; in fact, sometimes temptation seems even more powerful. God knows your weaknesses—maybe better than you do. He wants you to pray to Him when you are faced with temptation to sin.

Remember, you can be completely honest with God. You might as well—He already knows everything anyway. So when you face a difficult situation, ask God to help you not to be overcome.

Tell God Everything

Another important verse to learn about prayer comes from Paul's letter to the Philippians. Most people focus on the word *worry* in this verse but the word *pray* is just as important:

> *Don't worry about anything; instead, pray about everything. Tell God what you need, and thank him for all he has done. (Philippians 4:6)*

"Pray about everything." Did you know you can do that? You can talk to God about anything and everything.

The book of Nehemiah gives us a great study on the power and procedure of prayer. Nehemiah was cupbearer to the king of Persia. His family had been taken into exile, and Nehemiah had risen to this trusted position. Yet Nehemiah longed for Jerusalem. Like many other Jews, he missed living in their land and worshiping in their temple.

We read in Nehemiah 1:5-11 a prayer he prayed

upon receiving the news about the broken-down walls of the city of Jerusalem:

> *Then I said, "O Lord, God of heaven, the great and awesome God who keeps his covenant of unfailing love with those who love him and obey his commands, listen to my prayer! Look down and see me praying night and day for your people Israel. I confess that we have sinned against you. Yes, even my own family and I have sinned! We have sinned terribly by not obeying the commands, laws, and regulations that you gave us through your servant Moses.*
>
> *Please remember what you told your servant Moses: 'If you sin, I will scatter you among the nations. But if you return to me and obey my commands, even if you are exiled to the ends of the earth, I will bring you back to the place I have chosen for my name to be honored.'*
>
> *We are your servants, the people you rescued by your great power and might. O Lord, please hear my prayer! Listen to the prayers of those of us who delight in honoring you. Please grant me success now as I go to ask the king for a great favor. Put it into his heart to be kind to me."*

Notice the pattern of Nehemiah's prayer. Although he was weeping, his first words glorify and acknowledge God (just as in the Lord's Prayer). Notice the confession of sin on behalf of his people. Then finally, at the end, he presents his request. And what a request!

He was going to ask the king for a leave of absence from his job as cupbearer to go to Jerusalem and head up the rebuilding of the city's walls. This was quite a sacrifice on Nehemiah's part. A cupbearer had access to the king and was in a position of influence and power. Yet the people of God needed help, and Nehemiah was in a position to do something. So he did!

Then notice something else. Nehemiah is still grieving, trying to figure out what to do, when the king notices that he looks sad and asks him about it. The Bible says that Nehemiah "was badly frightened" (Nehemiah 2:2). Why? Well, in that culture the king could have a person killed for just looking sad in his presence. But what did Nehemiah do? He explained why he was sad. The king offered to help, and "with a prayer to the God of heaven" (v. 4), Nehemiah spelled out his request (he'd obviously thought this through very carefully).

Nehemiah gives us an example of a long prayer in a time of deep conversation with God and a quick prayer in a time of immediate need. Nehemiah could pray a quick prayer because he already had a foundation of fervent and honest prayer to God.

Tell God everything when you pray. Tell God the big needs and the little needs. Spend time with God in lengthy conversations and then you'll be able to send up short SOS prayers at a moment's notice. God is always listening, so always pray!

Never Give Up

How important it is that we learn the value of praying persistently. Some say you should only pray about something once—to pray about it again would show a lack of faith. I don't believe this is what Scripture teaches us.

Before He went to the cross, Jesus prayed more than once, "Let this cup of suffering be taken away from me" (Matthew 26:39, 42, 44). The apostle Paul prayed three times for the Lord to heal an illness that seemed to be curtailing his ministry (see 2 Corinthians 12:8).

In Luke 18 Jesus told a parable highlighting this important aspect of prayer:

One day Jesus told his disciples a story to illustrate their need for constant prayer and to show them that they must never give up. "There was a judge in a certain city," he said, "who was a godless man with great contempt for everyone. A widow of that city came to him repeatedly, appealing for justice against someone who had harmed her. The judge ignored her for a while, but eventually she wore him out. 'I fear neither God nor man,' he said to himself, 'but this woman is driving me crazy. I'm going to see that she gets justice, be-

cause she is wearing me out with her constant requests!'"

Then the Lord said, "Learn a lesson from this evil judge. Even he rendered a just decision in the end, so don't you think God will surely give justice to his chosen people who plead with him day and night? Will he keep putting them off? I tell you, he will grant justice to them quickly! But when I, the Son of Man, return, how many will I find who have faith?" (Luke 18:1-8)

In 1 Thessalonians 5:17-18 we are reminded to "pray without ceasing, in everything give thanks; for this is the will of God in Christ Jesus for you" (NKJV).

Sometimes God's timing is not ours. In fact, *often* God's timing is not ours. Even so, we should be persistent—pray without ceasing. God never gets tired of hearing our requests; He never leaves the answering machine on to screen out our persistent calls. He encourages us to keep on praying, always trusting that He will answer in His way, in His time.

Be Bold and Confident

James tell us not to doubt that God will answer our prayers:

If you need wisdom—if you want to know what God wants you to do—ask him, and he will gladly tell you. He will not resent your asking. But when you ask him, be sure that you really expect him to answer, for a doubtful mind is as unsettled as a wave of the sea that is driven and tossed by the wind. People like that should not expect to receive anything from the Lord. They can't make up their minds. They waver back and forth in everything they do. (James 1:5-8)

You may feel new at this, but don't worry. Right from the start, pray with confidence. There is nothing wrong with being bold and confident in your prayers. In fact, you should be.

Jesus gave His followers these promises about prayer:

Listen to me! You can pray for anything, and if you believe, you will have it. (Mark 11:24)

I also tell you this: If two of you agree down here on earth concerning anything you ask, my Father in heaven will do it for you. (Matthew 18:19)

So, you might be wondering, *I can pray for lots of money, and it will come? I can pray to win that promotion or get into that school or get a new car, and it will just happen? I can pray for someone to be healed, and he will be healed? I can pray about anything, and if I believe, I will get it?*

Well, yes and no.

As with any verse of Scripture, you always have to read all that Jesus said on the topic—not taking your entire theology from one verse. And then you must always read what is said before and after that verse. It's called reading in context.

As a new believer, you will grow in your knowledge of God by reading His Word. The more you learn about Him, the more you'll understand what the Bible calls "the mind of Christ." You'll seek God's desires above your own when you pray. After all, *you* may think that what you desire is the very best thing—but God may have other plans.

In the next chapter we will look further into what it means to pray with confidence, expecting God to answer.

4

EXPECTING GOD'S ANSWERS

God has promised to answer our prayers—but He's never said the answer will always be yes! As human beings we will never be able to fathom God and His ways. He sees the big picture; He knows what good can come out of bad situations; He knows certain bad things need to come to strengthen our character or prepare us for a future task. So even when we pray for what we think is God's will, we need to allow God to do His work, in His way, in His time.

When God Says No

Sometimes, no matter how well intentioned your prayer, God will say no. That happened to Paul. This great apostle traveled across much of the Roman Empire, fearlessly taking the gospel into cities where he was laughed at, beaten, jailed, and once even stoned and left for dead. But Paul had a problem; he called it a "thorn in [the] flesh" (2 Corinthians 12:7). We don't know for sure what the problem was. Some commentators believe it had to do with his eyes, because when he wrote to the Galatians he said, "I know you would gladly have taken out your own eyes and given them to me if it had been possible" (Galatians 4:15).

Paul had an entire world he wanted to reach for Christ. Doesn't it make sense that he would pray for God to take his disability away so he could be even more effective in his ministry?

It was a prayer that made perfect sense and certainly, it seemed to Paul, was in line with God's will. His motivation in asking for healing was so he could be more effective in ministry.

But God said no. Each time He said, "My gracious favor is all you need. My power works best in your weakness" (2 Corinthians 12:9).

God made it clear that He knew better than Paul. What was the reason? Paul explained that one reason was to keep him from getting too proud. His "thorn" reminded him that everything he accomplished was by God's grace and strength.

Maybe another reason was that God knew His busy messenger needed rest once in a while—and he'd only take it if it was forced on him. Whatever the case, God knew best, and His answer was no.

When God Says Wait

Sometimes you will get a yes, but the answer may not be visible for many years—in essence, you are getting a "wait." For example, God may say, "Yes, I will bring that person into my kingdom," but you may wait many years to see it happen.

Remember, time is very different with God. The Bible says, "You must not forget, dear friends, that a day is like a thousand years to the Lord, and a thousand years is like a day" (2 Peter 3:8). So you may be waiting for years and years while, according to God, He answered the very day you asked!

The "wait" answer can be very difficult because we want to see results. At times we think that God just didn't hear us. But remember the parable Jesus taught about prayer. He said keep on praying; never give up; be persistent.

Sometimes the answer God gives is totally unexpected. Look at the example of Zechariah, father of John the Baptist. Zechariah served as a priest in Israel. Back in Old Testament times, King David had made up a schedule so priests from all over Israel could come for a couple of weeks at a time to serve in God's temple in Jerusalem. One priest was chosen by lot (like drawing straws) to actually enter the Holy Place in the temple to burn incense each morning. This was a great honor and probably a once-in-a-lifetime opportunity.

Well, one particular morning when Zechariah's division (called the Abijah division) was on duty, the lot fell to Zechariah. "As was the custom of the priests, he was chosen by lot to enter the sanctuary and burn incense in the Lord's presence" (Luke 1:9). So he went into the Holy Place, and an angel appeared and said, "Don't be afraid, Zechariah! For God has heard your prayer, and your wife, Elizabeth, will bear you a son! And you are to name him John" (Luke 1:13).

What did the angel mean? Was Zechariah in the Holy Place praying for his wife to have a son? I doubt it. Most likely he was praying for the promised Messiah to come and deliver his nation—that would be the appropriate prayer for a priest who entered the Holy Place. But surely Zechariah had prayed many, many times that he and Elizabeth would have a child. Since the Bible tells us they were old and well past the age of childbearing, my guess is that they had stopped praying that prayer some time ago.

Now, unexpectedly, after years of thinking God was saying no, Zechariah and Elizabeth realized that His answer had really been "wait." He had finally said yes to their prayer for a child. And at the same time, God was also answering the prayer for the coming of the Messiah, for which Zechariah and the people in the temple were probably praying (see Luke 1:10). The coming of Zechariah's child was one link in the answer to the prayers of an entire nation, for that child, John the Baptist, would be the messenger to announce the Messiah.

God will answer your prayers, but many times His answers will surprise you. Often they will be so much better than you could have dreamed up yourself. Sometimes you'll sense a touch of humor in His answers. And you'll discover that His timing was much better than the timing you had wanted.

When you pray, be ready! The answers may come in the most unexpected ways.

Joined to Jesus

Jesus gave us an incredible promise about answering prayer:

> *If you stay joined to me and my words remain in you, you may ask any request you like, and it will be granted! (John 15:7)*

Literally, Jesus was saying, "I command you to ask at once for yourselves whatsoever you desire. It's yours."

Quite a promise! But there are some conditions in that promise: "*If* you stay joined to me and my words remain in you." What does this mean?

To be "joined" to Jesus means to be living in continual fellowship with Him, like two friends who are comfortable in each other's presence. You are not ill at ease, looking forward to getting away from Him; instead, you look forward to being together, and you enjoy each other's company. This is what Jesus was implying when He said, "Look! Here I stand at the door and knock. If you hear me calling and open the door, I will come in, and we will share a meal as friends" (Revelation 3:20).

Being joined to Jesus pictures intimate friendship.

That means that everything you do and every choice you make revolves around Jesus. It means that He has a say in everything you do. It means that you seek always to glorify Him in your life.

Remember that this intimacy must be balanced with a healthy reverence and awe of who God is. We are not to become too cavalier with God, either. I live in southern California—the capital of casual. Many people carry their casual outlook toward life into the church, their relationship with God, and their prayer lives. God is almighty, and He is to be revered, worshiped, and obeyed.

The way you live has a lot to do with how your prayers are answered. If you are practicing a sin, your prayers will go nowhere. Notice that I did not say, "If you ever sin, your prayers will go nowhere." No—of course you will sin every day. But if you are holding on to something that you know is a sin, and you refuse to stop doing it, you can't expect God to answer your prayers. Why not? Because if you aren't listening to what He has already told you, He's not going to say any more to you. The psalmist says, "If I had cherished sin in my heart, the Lord would not have listened" (Psalm 66:18, NIV).

When you're joined to Jesus, you will always seek to glorify Him, to put Him first in everything. There is a story in the Bible of a man who came to Jesus and wanted to follow Him. But the man said, "Lord, first let me return home and bury my father" (Matthew 8:21).

The wrong here is not that the man needed to attend a funeral; the point is that he wanted to follow Jesus, but not until his father had passed away. Maybe he was afraid if he took off with Jesus, he'd lose his inheritance or his reputation or whatever. To say "Lord" and then "first let me" is an oxymoron. (You know what that is, don't you? That's when words that are actually opposites are put together, like *jumbo shrimp, genuine imitation,* or *freezer burn.*)

Many people have the attitude that they can follow God tomorrow or when it's more convenient. But if you're joined to Christ, you can't say "me first"; this must be reflected in your prayers.

Your prayers are not a grocery list of things you need or want; if they were, you might as well pray to "our Santa in heaven" or "our butler in heaven." No, your prayers are part of your relationship with God. Prayer is two-way communication: you talk; you listen. Chances are, God will say a whole lot more to you than you might have thought! Prayer is about being joined to Jesus. It's about putting Him first.

His Word in You

In the second part of John 15:7, Jesus says, "[If] my words remain in you, you may ask any request you like, and it will be granted!" What does this mean about your prayers?

To have God's words remain in you means that God's Word is at home in your heart. This means, therefore, that your prayers cannot be divorced from your lifestyle. Your prayers flow out of a close walk with God. If your life is not pleasing to God, your prayer life will be ineffective, inconsistent, and maybe even nonexistent.

Obedience plays an important part in answered prayers:

> *We will receive whatever we request because we obey him and do the things that please him.* (1 John 3:22)

In other words, if we give a listening ear to all God's commands to us, He will give a listening ear to all our prayers to Him.

A big part of this is understanding *to whom* you are praying. The best way to learn more about God is to read His Word—the entire Bible—and see who He is and what He has done.

Read in Genesis how He created this beautiful world. Watch how sin enters the picture and how God immediately sets into place a plan to deal with it. See how He chose a man—Abraham—to be the father of a nation through whom the Messiah, the Savior, would come. Read about all the people in Genesis who disappointed God but through whom God continued to work because of His promise. And watch how He changed their lives. Imperfect people; a perfect God. God has a plan that stretches from eternity past to eternity future. God knows everything.

Read in Exodus the story of great evil in the world in the form of an Egyptian pharaoh who subdued God's people and killed their children. Watch God miraculously setting His people free from slavery— first wreaking havoc in the land of the Egyptians by showing each of their gods to be powerless. (The sun god cannot stop the darkness; the god of the Nile cannot keep the river from turning to blood; the god of the cattle cannot keep them from dying.) God is all-powerful.

Study the laws God gave to His nation so that they could live in harmony with Him and with each other. God is perfect and holy.

Watch these imperfect people, just set free from slavery, complaining about living in the desert and wanting to go back to Egypt! Watch God deal kindly with them again and again; watch Him exact punishment when it is deserved. Sin has consequences, and God is a just judge.

Read about the Israelites finally receiving the land God promised to Abraham. God keeps His promises. He is faithful.

Read about the glory days under David and Solomon. Read the tragic stories of the kings. Study the prophets who consistently brought God's messages to the people during the time of the kings—some were listened to, most weren't. Yet God in His love sent warnings to His people, second chances (and third and fourth). God is compassionate.

Read about how God's Son came to earth to die for people—to take away the punishment our sins deserve. God is love.

Study the letters of the New Testament that show Christianity in action. Learn how to make your faith work in your daily life. God is good.

Absorb the book of Revelation that gives a glimpse of the future. One day, sin and evil will be completely vanquished and God's people will live with Him forever. God is supreme and sovereign.

The more you learn about God, the more you'll understand the Power to whom you are praying. When you think of the "bigness" of God, you will see the "smallness" of your problems in comparison. As Scripture says, "Is anything too hard for the Lord?" (Genesis 18:14).

When God's Word remains in you—that is, as you study and learn more about God and His workings with His people—you'll understand how to obey Him. With His Word in your heart, you'll know how to pray, and you can trust God to answer.

Good Gifts

"Okay," you say, "I trust that God will answer, but I'm afraid of what He might say!" Many people are afraid that if they say to God, "I trust you with my life; I'll serve you completely," God will immediately send them to the place they least want to go—the deepest jungles of Africa, perhaps. But let's look at what Jesus says:

Keep on asking, and you will be given what you ask for. Keep on looking, and you will find. Keep on knocking, and the door will be opened. For everyone who asks, receives. Everyone who seeks, finds. And the door is opened to everyone who knocks. You parents—if your children ask for a loaf of bread, do you give them a stone instead? Or if they ask for a fish, do you give them a snake? Of course not! If you sinful people know how to give good gifts to your children, how much more will your heavenly Father give good gifts to those who ask him. (Matthew 7:7-11)

When your beautiful child comes to you and asks for a sandwich for lunch, you're not going to serve up poisonous snakes and think it's a big joke. And you're just a sinful human being! You love your children, so you try to always do what's best; you'd never intentionally hurt them or put them in danger.

Well, God is your perfect heavenly Father. When you come to Him with your humble heart, desiring to serve Him, He's not going to make you suffer as part of some big cosmic joke. He wants to make use of every gift He's given you—as well as your background, your experiences, what you enjoy—and wrap them into a big gift called your future.

Sure, He may send you in some unexpected directions, but you'll discover that serving Him will be your greatest fulfillment. You'll do things you never dreamed you could do; you'll accomplish for God acts that you never would have imagined. How? Because you let God work through you to build His kingdom.

Listen to God's declaration of His love for you:

For I know the thoughts that I think toward you, says the Lord, thoughts of peace and not of evil, to give you a future and a hope. Then you will call upon Me and go and pray to Me, and I will listen to you. And you will seek Me and find Me, when you search for Me with all your heart. I will be found by you, says the Lord. (Jeremiah 29:11-14, NKJV)

God's plans for you are good, not bad. He has a particular goal in mind for you. Take the time to contemplate His glory and character. Spend time in His presence through prayer. Begin to walk in His unique and wonderful plan for your life.

It will be the adventure of a lifetime!

5

IF GOD ALREADY KNOWS,
WHY PRAY?

Now that's a really good question. One of the first things you have learned about God is the fact that He is omniscient—meaning He knows everything. He knows the past, He knows the future, He knows your deepest, hidden (or so you thought) motives and desires. He knows your worries and fears. He knows your words before you say them. As the psalmist said:

> *O Lord, you have examined my heart and know everything about me. You know when I sit down or stand up. You know my every thought when far away. . . . You know what I am going to say even before I say it, Lord. . . . You saw me before I was born. Every day of my life was recorded in your book. Every moment was laid out before a single day had passed. (Psalm 139:1-2, 4, 16)*

And consider Jesus' words:

> *Your Father knows exactly what you need even before you ask him! (Matthew 6:8)*

So if God already knows what you're going to say, if He knows your needs before you ask, if He already knows what's going to happen anyway—then why bother to pray?

Pray Because Jesus Told You To

When Jesus was on earth, He prayed to His Father—even though His Father obviously already knew everything He would need.

In the garden of Gethsemane, Jesus spoke directly to God, pleading for Him to take away the cup of suffering, yet willing to complete the task God had given Him (see Mark 14:36; Luke 22:42). Before Jesus raised Lazarus from the dead, He first spoke to God: "Jesus looked up to heaven and said, 'Father, thank you for hearing me. You always hear me, but I said it out loud for the sake of all these people standing here, so they will believe you sent me.' Then Jesus shouted, 'Lazarus, come out!'" (John 11:41-43). When Jesus fed the five thousand, He collected a small amount of food from a young boy, "looked up toward heaven, and asked God's blessing on the food. Breaking the loaves into pieces, he gave some of the bread and fish to each disciple, and the disciples gave them to the people" (Matthew 14:19). Some mothers brought their children to Jesus, "so he could lay his hands on them and pray for them" (Matthew 19:13).

Jesus did not pray in order to impress people; in fact, that was one of the problems He saw with the religious leaders. Jesus seemed to take it for granted that He needed to pray to God in order to receive His answers. If it was that way for Jesus, it is most certainly the case with us!

Yes, we should pray simply because Jesus told us to. Even if it were extremely difficult to do (which it's not), or very unpleasant (which it isn't), or if we never got answers (which we do), we should pray because we are commanded to pray.

Pray Because It Is God's Plan for You

It is important to remember that prayer is not about changing God; it's about changing *you!* It's not about having to plead with God, wrestle with Him, instruct Him, or bend His arm to help you when He really doesn't want to. No, prayer is about talking to a God who truly cares about you. He *wants* to help you. True praying is not overcoming God's reluctance but laying hold of His willingness! Martin Luther said, "By our praying, we are instructing ourselves more than Him."

Prayer is God's appointed way for obtaining things. The Bible says, "The reason you don't have what you want is that you don't ask God for it" (James 4:2).

You might ask, "Why is it that I don't seem to know God's will for my life?"

"The reason you don't have what you want is that you don't ask God for it."

"Why am I still struggling so much with certain sins?"

"The reason you don't have what you want is that you don't ask God for it."

"Why do I still face so many job and financial worries?"

"The reason you don't have what you want is that you don't ask God for it."

Jesus came that we might be able to have a relationship with His Father. Sin separated us from God, but Jesus died in our place, thereby satisfying the righteous demand of a holy God against whom we all have sinned.

As we realize that truth, turn from our sin, and put our faith in Jesus Christ as our Savior and Lord, we become God's children. And an integral part of our new relationship with God includes communication. We don't have relationships with people we never talk to. A true relationship includes some give-and-take. Sometimes we talk and they listen, and sometimes it's the other way around. But we wouldn't have a relationship with someone who only talked or only listened. It has to be a two-way street.

Likewise, in order to have a relationship with God, you need to communicate with Him. The only way to communicate is through prayer. That will often include asking, because we are frail human beings who desperately need God's help in order to live our lives in ways that please Him.

Communication also means listening. What does it mean to "listen" to God? How do you do that? In order to hear God, you need to learn to tune in to what He is saying. Jesus often said, "If anyone has ears to hear, let him hear" (Mark 4:23, NIV).

It would be a great idea to somehow get away to a quiet place, as Jesus often did, retreat from the noisy crowds, and wait on the Father in prayer. It could also be as simple as turning off your cell phone and car radio when in your vehicle and just speaking and listening to God. (Make sure you keep your eyes open!)

Through those quiet times you will come to know His voice. You will come to understand how He speaks to you. In those times, as you search His Word for guidance—and then listen—you will begin to "hear" His voice. This is not some mystical, out-of-this-world event; it is simply the reality of God's Holy Spirit at work in your life. You will hear God's voice through Christian friends, your pastor, or through certain events. You'll recognize it as you become more familiar with God's work in your life.

God does not leave you to your own devices. He calls you to come to Him with your desires, your requests, your needs. Just as you would want your children to come to you with whatever is on their minds, so God wants that from you.

Pray Because It Helps You

What a God we have who plans a way for us to communicate with Him! For Christians, prayer is a joyous part of our relationship with Him. Here are a few ways prayer helps us:

- Prayer helps us to keep our dependence upon God.

- Prayer helps us to get our perspective back—especially when we come to prayer first adoring God, then confessing our sins, then thanking Him, and finally presenting our needs to Him in supplication. (Remember ACTS?)

- Prayer helps us overcome anxiety and worry. We looked at this verse previously, but it is worth noting again: "Don't worry about anything; instead, pray about everything. Tell God what you need, and thank him for all he has done" (Philippians 4:6).

- Prayer helps us to resist Satan and his temptations. "For we are not fighting against people made of flesh and blood, but against the evil rulers and authorities of the unseen world, against those mighty powers of darkness who rule this world, and against wicked spirits in the heavenly realms. . . . Pray at all times and on every occasion in the power of the Holy Spirit. Stay alert and be persistent in your prayers for all Christians everywhere" (Ephesians 6:12, 18).

- Prayer helps us to see the will of God more clearly.

What a blessing God gave us when He gave us prayer!

Pray Because It Prepares You for Jesus' Return

Prayer is one of the ways in which we make ourselves ready for Christ's return.

Be always on the watch, and pray that you may be able to escape all that is about to happen, and that you may be able to stand before the Son of Man. (Luke 21:36, NIV; emphasis mine)

But of that day and hour no one knows, not even the angels in heaven, nor the Son, but only the Father. Take heed, watch and pray; for you do not know when the time is. (Mark 13:32-33, NKJV; emphasis mine)

Jesus is going to come back—He promised that to us! In the meantime, we are to live for Him on this planet. His goal is to make us "mature and complete, not lacking anything" (James 1:4, NIV). Why? Because He is preparing us for heaven. And we want to be ready!

Perhaps one of the most poignant pictures of our need for prayer comes from C. S. Lewis. In the book *The Magician's Nephew* (one of the Chronicles of Narnia), two children are sent by Aslan (the figure of Christ in the story) to do an important task. They are transported by a flying horse named Fledge, and when they land for the night, the children are very hungry. Fledge is quite surprised at this, for he did not know that children do not eat grass.

One of them, Digory, said, "Well, I *do* think someone might have arranged about our meals."

"I'm sure Aslan would have, if you'd asked him," said Fledge.

"Wouldn't he know without being asked?" said Polly.

"I've no doubt he would," said the horse (still with his mouth full). "But I've a sort of idea he likes to be asked."

Our God likes to be asked. So ask.

6

Obstacles to Effective Prayer

Prayer is an awesome privilege. Prayer is your lifeline to God. Prayer is your vehicle for staying close to Him and living in line with His will for you.

So guess what? Satan doesn't like it. In fact, he hates it. He hates the fact that you can receive guidance from God and stay on the right pathway for your life. He hates the fact that God comes to help you when you call on Him in times of difficulty and temptation. He hates your quiet time when you meditate on all God has done for you. As an old hymn of the church says, "Satan trembles when he sees the weakest saint upon his knees."

His "end game" is to destroy you in any way he can. But he also recognizes that you have committed your life to Christ and are under divine protection—so his second-best plan is to immobilize you. And one of the best ways to do this is to stop you from praying.

In this chapter we will look at some of the things that can go wrong in a Christian's prayer life—not to worry you or cause you alarm, but just to make you aware of potential pitfalls you may face.

The Problem of Pride

Who would think that during something as spiritual as the act of prayer we could be capable of sin? Jesus shows very clearly that this is not only possible, it can really be a problem. Even while praying we can be guilty of hypocrisy and self-centeredness—the sin of *pride.*

Jesus told a parable of a Pharisee (a religious leader) and a tax collector (a despised Jewish person who collected taxes for the Romans):

> *Two men went to the Temple to pray. One was a Pharisee, and the other was a dishonest tax collector. The proud Pharisee stood by himself and prayed this prayer: "I thank you, God, that I am not a sinner like everyone else, especially like that tax collector over there! For I never cheat, I don't sin, I don't commit adultery, I fast twice a week, and I give you a tenth of my income." But the tax collector stood at a distance and dared not even lift his eyes to heaven as he prayed. Instead, he beat his chest in sorrow, saying, "O God, be merciful to me, for I am a sinner." I tell you, this sinner, not the Pharisee, returned home justified before God. For the proud will be humbled, but the humble will be honored. (Luke 18:10-14)*

The Pharisee had the reputation of a man of God; the tax collector had the reputation of a turncoat, a traitor, and a greedy, dishonest cheat. Pharisees were admired; tax collectors were scorned. Many of them not only collected the taxes Rome required but added more to the amounts they collected and kept it for themselves (that was legal—Rome didn't care as long as it got its cut).

So here we have this Pharisee and this tax collector—almost like saying a minister and a drug dealer—going into a church to pray. You get the idea. Now, immediately you might think that the Pharisee (or the minister) has the direct line to God. God will obviously hear and answer this holy man. But Jesus throws us a curve (as He often does!).

The problem was that the Pharisee wasn't praying to talk to God at all; he was praying to be heard and admired by those around him. He was actually bragging about his accomplishments in prayer! Jesus declared that it was not the Pharisee's but the tax collector's prayer that was heard—because he came in reverence to God, knowing he was a sinner who needed mercy.

Jesus spoke at other times about religious leaders who would "pray publicly on street corners and in the synagogues where everyone can see them" (Matthew 6:5). Apparently, their public prayers—maybe long-winded and self-congratulatory—made people think that they were really holy people. But because their prayers were meant more for the people to hear than for God to hear, Jesus explained that the praise of the people was "all the reward they will ever get."

You will have private times of prayer with God, and you will have times of corporate prayer with other believers—either in small groups where you may pray aloud or in groups where you are simply joining with others in prayer. Both are important. But it's interesting to note when reading the Gospels that Jesus' prayers were short when offered in public and very lengthy when He was alone with God. He could spend a whole night in communion with His Father.

How different with so many believers. Many have short prayers in private but long prayers in public. Perhaps some people pray such long prayers in front of others because, like the Pharisees, they want to impress people with their devotion to God. But it doesn't impress God, and He is the one to whom prayer should be addressed.

When you want to have a heart-to-heart talk with someone, would you do it with an audience? If you would, what do you think would be your motive? When you want to have a serious talk with a friend, you do it privately, at a time when you won't be disturbed.

That's what your communication with God is like. There are times when you will pray with other believers, but those times of corporate prayer should come out of already having solid private time in prayer with God. Getting together with a group is not a substitute for private prayer.

And one more note: Besides the ones who are

praying long-winded prayers to impress people, you may come across some whose "prayer requests" are just thinly veiled gossip: "Lord, you know that Jim has been cheating at school and sleeping with his girl-friend, and we ask you to show him the right way"; or "Father, you know Ed has been having financial problems lately. . . ." You can discuss anything you want with God in private, but the words you pray publicly need to be carefully chosen.

Vain Repetitions

Another problem Jesus addressed was prayers that were ritualized, repeated over and over with little attention paid to what was said. He told His followers, "Don't babble on and on as people of other religions do. They think their prayers are answered only by repeating their words again and again" (Matthew 6:7).

Using prewritten prayers becomes a problem when we say them over and over as our only prayer. Why? Because if we aren't careful, we find ourselves reciting them without even thinking about what we're saying. "For this food we are about to receive . . ." you say; meanwhile, you're thinking about what you're going to do after dinner. What kind of praying is that?

Don't misunderstand. Written prayers are not bad in themselves. The point is that they should not be your only prayers.

Your prayer time can be—and should be—like

getting together with your very best friend to talk things over. You don't have the same conversation every time you meet!

Prayers That Go Nowhere

Most believers have times when they feel as though their prayers are "hitting the ceiling." Although God is certainly in all places at all times and always ready to listen to His children, Scripture makes it clear that there are things that get in the way of His answering.

Unconfessed Sin

The prophet Isaiah explained to the people,

> *Listen! The Lord is not too weak to save you, and he is not becoming deaf. He can hear you when you call. But there is a problem—your sins have cut you off from God. Because of your sin, he has turned away and will not listen anymore. (Isaiah 59:1-2)*

In chapter 4 we discussed this at some length. We looked at the psalmist's words, "If I had cherished sin in my heart, the Lord would not have listened" (Psalm 66:18, NIV).

Again, it's not that God expects you never to sin again. The problem arises when you know what you should do but don't do it; when you *cherish* sin in your heart; when you hold on to something that you know is a sin and refuse to give it up. If God is speaking to you about a sin you need to abandon, and you refuse to do so, then you can't expect that He's going to answer your prayers. In a way, you have terminated the conversation with Him.

Wrong Motives

James encourages us to look at the motives behind our prayers. "When you ask, you do not receive, because you ask with wrong motives, that you may spend what you get on your pleasures" (James 4:3, NIV).

Some might pray, "God, use me!" but deep down they want God to use them so that they can become famous and have people speak their name. Their motive is not God's glory, but their own.

Or a young man might pray, "Lord, save that girl!" not because he is concerned about her spiritual state, but because he has already become romantically involved with her, knowing she isn't a believer, and he feels guilty about it.

James didn't want us to be praying carelessly. We need to examine ourselves, making sure that our selfish desires do not contaminate our prayers. What is the motive behind your request? What will you do to glorify God if the Lord answers your prayer with a yes? Do you believe that what you are praying for is truly God's will? Is what you are requesting in the best interest of God's kingdom?

Idols in Our Lives

The prophet Ezekiel wrote,

> *Son of man, these leaders have set up idols in their*
> *hearts. They have embraced things that lead them*
> *into sin. Why should I let them ask me anything?*
> *(Ezekiel 14:3)*

You may be thinking, *This one's not about me. I don't bow down before any idols.*

But what is an idol? It is anything or anyone that takes the place of God in your life. An idol can be any object, idea, philosophy, habit, occupation, sport, or whatever has your primary concern and loyalty.

Our bodies can be idols if we spend all of our time and energy worrying about exercise or diet. If it gets in the way of our time with God ("I'll go to the gym at 5:00 A.M., but I won't have time for my prayer or Bible study"), it may have become an idol.

What about our jobs? Would we do anything to keep a certain job—even actions that would disappoint God? Do we allow our work to take over our lives to the degree that we don't have the time or energy to think about Him? Then our work is an idol.

What about our possessions? Are they so important to us that we could not give anything up if God wanted us to? Do we spend all of our time worrying about them to the point that we cannot trust in God to care for us? Or do we want certain possessions so much that we will do anything to get them? Are we so focused on the things we want that we can't think of anything else? Then our possessions (or the possessions we desire) are idols.

What about other people? Do we want them to think well of us, so we keep quiet about our faith? Are we afraid of what people might think? Perhaps some friends are dragging us down spiritually. Whenever we spend time with them, we are worse off for it. God warns us, "Do not follow the advice of the wicked" (Psalm 1:1). When we do, such people could become idols in our lives.

Until you deal with these things, your prayer life will not be what it ought to be.

Lack of Forgiveness

Forgiven people should be forgiving people. An unforgiving attitude is one of the most common hindrances to prayer. Are you nursing a grudge against someone? You need to let it go. After all, when you consider all that God has forgiven you, is that too much to ask?

Jesus told a parable about this:

The Kingdom of Heaven can be compared to a king who decided to bring his accounts up to date with servants who had borrowed money from him. In the process, one of his debtors was brought in who owed him millions of dollars. He couldn't pay, so the king ordered that he, his wife, his children, and everything he had be sold to pay the debt. But the man fell down before the king and begged him, "Oh, sir, be patient with me, and I will pay it all." Then the king was filled with pity for him, and he released him and forgave his debt.

But when the man left the king, he went to a fellow servant who owed him a few thousand dollars. He grabbed him by the throat and demanded instant payment. His fellow servant fell down before him and begged for a little more time. "Be patient and I will pay it," he pleaded. But his creditor wouldn't wait. He had the man arrested and jailed until the debt could be paid in full.

When some of the other servants saw this, they were very upset. They went to the king and told him what had happened. Then the king called in the man he had forgiven and said, "You evil servant! I forgave you that tremendous debt because you pleaded with me. Shouldn't you have mercy on your fellow servant, just as I had mercy on you?" Then the angry king sent the man to prison until he had paid every penny.

That's what my heavenly Father will do to you if you refuse to forgive your brothers and sisters in your heart. (Matthew 18:23-35)

God's forgiveness is unlimited; therefore, our forgiveness should be as well. When we don't forgive others, we are showing that we don't understand or appreciate the forgiveness that God has given us. And it hinders our ability to pray.

God desires to communicate with you, but have you "hung up" on Him? If so, it's time to redial His number.

First you must deal with the areas addressed in this chapter. Check your motives, confess your sins, make sure there are no idols in your life, and forgive those who have hurt you.

Listen to what God says to us: "Call to me and I will answer you and tell you great and unsearchable things you do not know" (Jeremiah 33:3, NIV).

7

PRAYER THAT PREVAILS

In this final chapter we're going to unlock some of the secrets of prayer that make use of its power and potential. Let's look at the book of Acts where we see the power of prayer in action.

After the apostles Peter and John had been threatened by the Jewish leaders to stop preaching about Jesus, they "found the other believers and told them what the leading priests and elders had said. Then all the believers were united as they lifted their voices in prayer" (Acts 4:23-24).

The early believers faced intense persecution. The Jewish leaders sought to keep them quiet. They seized Peter and John and put them in jail at one point, and at another time, they imprisoned all the apostles. Things came to a head when they actually stoned Stephen for proclaiming Jesus as Lord.

Acts 12 tells the story of a time when King Herod arrested some of the believers. The king wanted to "stay in good" with the Jewish leaders in Jerusalem, so he had James executed. (This was James, the

brother of John, and one of Jesus' earliest disciples.)
Being the consummate politician, Herod, when he
"saw how much this pleased the Jewish leaders, . . .
arrested Peter during the Passover celebration"
(Acts 12:3).

When the Jewish leaders had imprisoned the
apostles previously, they miraculously escaped, so
this time Herod took extra precautions. Peter was
under the guard of four squads of four soldiers
each—that's sixteen men guarding him! Herod
wanted to bring Peter out for public trial after the
Passover—hoping, surely, to have the same result
that had been accomplished with a previous pris-
oner named Jesus. He had executed James; Peter was
next.

So Peter was in prison, and what did the church
do? Boycott all products made in Rome as a protest?
Gather with swords to go down and try to take on the
Roman soldiers guarding him? No, the church used
its "secret weapon." The Bible tells us that "constant
prayer was offered to God for him by the church"
(Acts 12:5, NKJV).

All other doors may have been closed, but one re-
mained open—the door of prayer. The way to secure
release for Peter was through God by means of
prayer.

So often prayer is our last resort when it should be
our first! Let's see what Scripture says about the
prayers of these early followers of Jesus.

Prevailing Prayer Is Offered to God

Acts 12:5 says that prayer was "offered to God" (NKJV).

"Well, of course," you may say. "Isn't all prayer offered to God?"

No, actually, it isn't. Often when we pray, our minds are so taken up with the thought of what we need that there is very little thought of God Himself.

For prayer to be powerful and effective, there needs to be a recognition of the One to whom we are speaking. In chapter 2 we observed that the model prayer Jesus taught His followers began, "Our Father in heaven, hallowed be your name."

In other words, prevailing prayer begins with the concept of going into the presence of God, your Father in heaven, who is perfect, holy, and awesome.

Needless to say, if you are in a life-threatening situation, a hearty "HELP!" will suffice. But under normal circumstances, we need to slow down and contemplate just who this awesome God is that we are praying to. Prayer should never be taken for granted. It is a privilege. So when you come into God's presence, come with reverence and awe, deeply grateful that He invites you there, that He listens, and that He will answer.

Prevailing Prayer Is Passionate

Acts 12:5 says that the believers' prayers were "constant" (NKJV). Other versions say that they prayed "earnestly."

These believers were not flippant about their prayers on Peter's behalf. They didn't say, "Dear Lord, (yawn), please save Peter . . . or whatever (zzzzzz). . ."

No, these prayers were literally storming the gates of heaven. You can almost hear them praying with tears and in agony, worried that Peter would soon face the same fate that their dear friend James had just experienced. These people prayed passionately, "Dear Lord, DELIVER PETER!!!"

The word *passionate* speaks of a soul that is filled with intense desire. The same word is used of Jesus in Luke 22:44, "He prayed more earnestly, and his sweat was like drops of blood falling to the ground" (NIV).

Prayer that prevails with God is prayer into which we put our whole soul, stretching out toward Him in intense and agonizing desire. Many of our prayers have no power in them because there is no heart in them! If we put so little heart into our prayers, we cannot expect God to put much heart into answering them. God promises that His people will find Him when they search for Him with all their heart.

Prevailing Prayer Is Persistent

Prayer that prevails is persistent. This "constant" prayer of the believers probably continued through several days and nights. Peter was not released until the night before the planned trial, but the believers kept on praying—and they were still praying when Peter arrived on their doorstep!

Remember the story Jesus told of the woman who needed justice from the corrupt judge (see chapter 3)? The point of the parable is not that God is corrupt and we have to nag Him for answers to our prayers: "Lord, you better come through on this or you'll have *me* to deal with!"

Yet some people pray that way. They feel they have to convince God because He really doesn't care. Or they feel they have to pray louder or longer to get Him to pay attention. But that is pagan in nature. That's like the prophets of the false god Baal in the Old Testament calling loudly to him for hours on end. They shouted and even cut themselves with knives to get Baal's attention, but they couldn't (see 1 Kings 18).

No, our God is not like the corrupt judge. And no, He is not a silent and lifeless idol. Our God is the exact opposite. In fact, Jesus ends that parable by explaining that if even a corrupt judge will end up giving justice when someone is persistent, how much more will God's children receive what is right from their loving heavenly Father! "So don't be afraid, little flock. For it gives your Father great happiness to give you the Kingdom" (Luke 12:32).

We don't have to threaten God or wear Him out. We are not trying to overcome His reluctance; we are trying to take hold of His willingness. We are not trying to bend God our way but seeking to bend His way. We are not trying to get our will into heaven but to get His will on earth.

Prevailing Prayer Is Prayed with Faith

Clearly there is an important place for faith in our prayers. And, no doubt, there are many occasions where God's work has been hindered because of unbelief. Having stated that, it is important for us to realize that it will not always be *our* faith that brings answers; sometimes it will be the faith of others.

Mark 5 tells us the story of a woman who had been having a problem with bleeding for twelve years. She had been to many doctors, and no one had been able to heal her disease. But "she had heard about Jesus, so she came up behind him through the crowd and touched the fringe of his robe. For she thought to herself, 'If I can just touch his clothing, I will be healed.' Immediately the bleeding stopped, and she could feel that she had been healed!" (Mark 5:27-29).

Jesus noticed that someone had touched Him, for He "realized at once that healing power had gone out from him" (Mark 5:30), and He sought out the person who had touched Him for healing. When the woman admitted it, Jesus kindly said to her, "Daughter, your faith has made you well. Go in peace. You have been healed" (Mark 5:34).

In this woman's case, Jesus responded to *her* faith.

Matthew 8:5-13 tells us the story of a Roman centurion (a commander or officer in the Roman army). He came to Jesus to request healing for his servant. Jesus said that He would come, but the Roman commander said, "Lord, I am not worthy to have you come into my home. Just say the word from where you are, and my servant will be healed!" (v. 8). Jesus was astounded at such faith and answered, "What you have believed has happened" (v. 13).

In this man's case, it was *his* faith that Jesus honored, not the faith of the one who needed the healing touch.

Finally, there is the story of Lazarus in John 11. Lazarus was a friend of Jesus. When he died, Jesus went to raise him from the dead. But Lazarus could have no faith on his own behalf; he was dead. His sisters, Mary and Martha, had believed that Jesus could heal Lazarus, but once he was dead, their hope was gone. The religious leaders who came to comfort Mary and Martha wondered why Jesus had not come back sooner.

There was so much doubt that day that Jesus wept.

But God intervened mightily and raised Lazarus from the dead. In the case of Lazarus, it was not the faith of the one being touched or the faith of another on his or her behalf; it was simply God intervening despite the imperfect faith of His people.

And that's what God did for this group of believers. As you will see by the end of the story, they did not really believe God would intervene as mightily as He did! But God can use our imperfect prayers to do His perfect will.

Prayer Power

So what happened with that passionate, persistent, prayer offered to God on Peter's behalf?

Let's look at the rest of the story, recorded in Acts 12:6-19.

Peter was jailed but not worried. In fact, the night before the trial, Peter was chained between two soldiers—and he was *asleep!* Talk about calm in the midst of the storm! He was probably the only believer in town asleep that night.

The rest were praying.

Suddenly an angel appeared in the cell, woke Peter up (had to strike him, actually, because he was so sound asleep), and told him to get up and get dressed. Immediately, the chains fell from Peter's wrists.

The angel told Peter to follow, and he did. Peter thought he was seeing a vision as he was led out of the prison, past the first and second sets of guards, and through an iron gate that opened by itself to let him through. Then he walked to the end of the block, and the angel left him.

Peter suddenly realized that this was indeed real, so he went to the home of Mary, mother of John (Mark), where people were gathered together praying for him.

He knocked on the door, and a girl named Rhoda came to answer it. She heard Peter's voice and ran back into the house to tell everyone that the beloved apostle was at the door.

In the meantime she left poor old Peter standing outside in the cold!

The believers looked up from their fervent prayers

for Peter's deliverance and basically said, "Right, Rhoda. Nice try. You're crazy."

But the very answer to their prayer was outside knocking. Finally someone else got up and went to the door and discovered—PETER!

Look at how God changed the situation in Acts 12 as a result of prayer. In the beginning of the chapter, a seemingly all-powerful King Herod was wreaking havoc on the Christians in Jerusalem. He had on his side the power of Rome. He executed one of their own and imprisoned another. The situation appeared hopeless.

But the believers had the power of God on their side—and their secret weapon: prayer.

The chapter ends with the great King Herod giving a speech met with such adulation that the people called him a god. Herod absorbed the praise as if he deserved it, and God dealt with him so severely that he died a horrible death.

The chapter opens with Peter in prison and Herod triumphing; it closes with Herod dead, Peter free, and God triumphing.

A Final Word

I hope that, having heard all these stories of answered prayer, you are saying, "I want to learn how to pray to a God that powerful!"

Because you can. You are a child of God, so you have the awesome privilege of prayer.

You don't have to be perfect to pray. Listen to one more encouraging story, found in Mark 9:14-29. A man brought his demon-possessed son to Jesus, asking Jesus to cast out the demon. "The evil spirit often makes him fall into the fire or into water, trying to kill him. Have mercy on us and help us. Do something if you can," he said (v. 22).

To which Jesus responded, "What do you mean, 'If I can'? . . . Anything is possible if a person believes" (v. 23).

The father understood but truthfully acknowledged his greatest fear. He tearfully said to Jesus, "Lord, I believe; help my unbelief!" (Mark 9:24, NKJV).

Did Jesus respond, "Well, I'm sorry; that's just not enough"? No. Jesus answered the man's prayer and healed his son.

Pray with passion, persistence, and as much faith as you can muster. God knows you are an imperfect person. Just say to Him, "Lord, I believe; help my unbelief!"

And you know what? He'll answer that prayer too!